THE HERO CULT

Anissia

Changing the Love Pattern

Edward

Mona Lisa Pamphlets

The Hero Cult

The Pamphlets and Poems

The Trial

Yami

THE HERO CULT

ANNOTATIONS ON INSANITY

Peter Fritz Walter

Published by Sirius-C Media Galaxy LLC

3511 Silverside Road, Suite 105, Wilmington 19380, Delaware, USA

Set in Avenir Light and Trajan Pro

Designed by Peter Fritz Walter

ISBN 978-1-983410-24-6

Publishing Categories
Psychology / Social Psychology

Series Autobiographical and Poetic Writings, Vol. 5

Publisher Contact Information
publisher@sirius-c-publishing.com
http://sirius-c-publishing.com

Author Contact Information
pfw@peterfritzwalter.com

About Dr. Peter Fritz Walter
http://peterfritzwalter.com

Parallel to an international law career in Germany, Switzerland and the United States, Dr. Peter Fritz Walter (Pierre) focused upon fine art, cookery, astrology, musical performance, social sciences and humanities.

He started writing essays as an adolescent and received a high school award for creative writing and editorial work for the school magazine.

After finalizing his law diplomas, he graduated with an LL.M. in European Integration at Saarland University, Germany, in 1982, and with a Doctor of Law title from University of Geneva, Switzerland, in 1987.

He then took courses in psychology at the University of Geneva and interviewed a number of psychotherapists in Lausanne and Geneva, Switzerland. His interest was intensified through a hypnotherapy with an Ericksonian American hypnotherapist in Lausanne. This led him to the recovery and healing of his inner child.

After a second career as a corporate trainer and personal coach, Pierre retired in 2004 as a full-time writer, philosopher and consultant.

His nonfiction books emphasize a systemic, holistic, cross-cultural and interdisciplinary perspective, while his fiction works and short stories focus upon education, philosophy, perennial wisdom, and the poetic formulation of an integrative worldview.

Pierre is a German-French bilingual native speaker and writes English as his 4th language after German, Latin and French. He also reads source literature for his research works in Spanish, Italian, Portuguese, and Dutch. In addition, Pierre has notions of Thai, Khmer, Chinese, Japanese, and Vietnamese.

All of Pierre's books are hand-crafted and self-published, designed by the author. Pierre publishes via his Delaware company, Sirius-C Media Galaxy LLC, and under the imprints of IPUBLICA and SCM (Sirius-C Media).

CONTENTS

PREFACE

Love is never respectable, said Krishnamurti.

If your love disturbs nobody, it's no love. *Your goodness must have some edge to it— else it is none*, said Emerson.

Loving young girls was a constant over the entire course of human history, and it was considered the purest, most noble, and most virtuous love of all loves.

And then, with *Puritanism* coming up as an antithesis to *Life*, love was declared a *perversion*; today puritanism is forgotten, and the perversion became the constant: the perversion of life in the form of standard opinions, television gossip, and *scientific authorities*.

The lover does not look down on the masses of putrefied souls, those who are *crippled emotionally, mentally, and sexually.* He knows that they are dead.

Instead he looks ahead.

Every generation of little girls comes with enough revolting seeds, enough truly female courage, enough civil disobedience, enough sensuality to *blow them all off to hell*, the *eternal* pharisaics, the *eternal* police asses, the *eternal* homo fuckers and coward oedipal *pissoir* suckers and the *eternal* good-boys-to-their moms.

Introduction

This text is written not by a virgin soul and love dreamer. I was one of those fortunate enough to lose virginity in childhood. Not written either by one of those who compose softer stuff, nicer little pamphlets, where the Biblical *manna* in the form of tiny virgins falls from heaven, and where the sun is shining eternally like in Disneyland.

I do not live in the new nirvana populated with heroes and heroines that label themselves as *pedophiles*. Others may better fit, with their *Peter Pan* makeup, and their home-made paranoia. I was not forbidden to talk *strong words* as a child. As a result, I am not one of these poetically diluted souls, filled with water, and drunken with fantasy.

I can talk *straight*. They are poets of a watery world that is since long forgotten, Atlantis. *I am a poet of hic et nunc.* They have the hero spirit, I have the Zen spirit.

Flat they are, one-dimensional robot souls, narcissistic, unable to see the *details* of life, of love.

You will not find *one* authentic love story in their cluttered pretentious lives, one true and lively relationship with its natural ups and downs.

They say they're *beyond that.* They say they're *the heroes of a world to come.* They say they're the *new men.* They are busy with their pamphlets of shiny morality, honor and virtue, of knights and of dukes, and Robin Hoods, and their diaries are sparkling with brazen statements. They indulge in the sentimental worship of exotic goddesses with tiny feet, and, you could guess it, who are bound to be *blond and blue-eyed.*

Their rhetorically minted juice is the smear that hides what they hide to themselves: their *desire.* For they have for the most part *no love experience* and go through their lives uncopulated, unpenetrated, unrelated, unpartnered. And then they eloquently preach eternal *virginity* as a *strange form of sainthood*, promoting as *fashionable* a life of desertation, not of penetration. *They have their degrees in bystandership.*

Their inner observer is hypertrophied and their spontaneity dead. They are talkers, not doers, cliché, pretenders.

They know all the should and ought-to that ever can be learnt in Sunday school; they know the Bible *by heart.* They know how many steps there are from home to Church, and from Church back home.

They are fake. And as fake, they ghost around and make the world believe they were this-and-that. Heroes. Heroines. Princes. Princesses. While their nobility is not of blue blood, but of *no* blood. They are dried pepper. Abrasive for the palate.

Brazen knights and fairies, they are chatting their souls off, unable to really get involved *for one time*, to say what they feel, for one time, to stand up for what they think, for one time. They are volatile, and never-to-catch. Eternal opportunists. Their heroism is a shield around their heart.

What brazen, silver, golden and platinum examples of alkaline fake in a fake culture! They defy fake by being *proactive* fake, by *incarnating* fake. Cultural heroes they are. Men and women who have achieved the *private victory* and then the *public victory*.

Tin soldiers.

They embody what America needs. Marching forward, strong in the mind, strong in the chest, icy statues of frigid virtue! I'd not be surprised to hear one day that one of them, that today declares himself being a *good pedophile*, is tomorrow a presidential candidate.

The tragic contradiction that splits them apart is their karma, their dharma, their drama, their theatrical mission. They show society that schizophrenia can be lived without hurt, and without running around amok. They are elegant. They are *distinguished*. They lead chaotic lives, but have *style* in their chaos.

They have their place in the *hero culture* that has brought them about and sustains them graciously.

It's probably because they are too nice and I am too naughty that we barely get along. But their niceties are covering their explosive passions that one day may turn against them. For the selves we disown one day come to haunt us.

Where is their Dionysus? Where is their Minotaur? Where is their shadow? Stored away. Hidden in a maze. Veiled behind a sunshine smile.

This book is written in a different style, vibrating at a different frequency, not infected by their insane sentimentality, and it shares an altogether different *Weltanschauung*. It is blunt, erect and naked. Less in the style of Church gospels, but more in the fashion of gypsy music.

This is the style that I will apply to my journey into *postmodern hero culture*. And in between, so to say for entertainment, I shall present some spicy interludes of wine and roses, or rather smelly little presents from the mouth of the court jester and that will hopefully upset you.

THE MUTE HERO

The *Mute Hero* has lost his tongue or never acquired a real, and genuine, vocabulary. He's been the pussy to *Her-Majesty-Your-Mom.*

She wanted him to shut up, to *slut up*, and be a *good boy*. She asked him to be silent. She wanted him to be dead. A child that is asked to be silent and quiet *all the time* is a dead child. Most children are murdered by their mothers.

Culture is created by language and culture is *none* when and where language is banned. He knew that, which is why he grew out of culture.

There was a silent taboo between him and Her Majesty, he sensed. She had nobody to share her bed. She was not fucked. A woman that is not fucked turns *foul*. If that happens to *Her-Majesty-Your-Mother*, that's even worse.

Taboos that prohibit language are not only impeding communication, but they destroy culture. He knew his relationship with Mom was *too close*, not physically, in the contrary; but their *minds* were fusioned. It was not his choice to be so close to her. He wanted to go *off, off and away*, to have more autonomy, but she would not let him.

He knew it was her problem, that she was symbiotoholic, *because she had no fucker*. All women who have no fucker become stale, rotten, neurotic, dreadful, a real pain in the ass.

But all of this, impossible to talk about it. He was afraid to mention any of this, while he *knew* it all. As a little boy. So he had to be the *Mute Hero*.

The prohibition of talk molds mute humans, people who have to use other forms of communication than verbal expression. They resort to violence as the only language that is not coded in words. *It's coded in hits.*

But he did not want to become violent, so he repressed all his aggressiveness. He became too polite, too good to be true, too gentle, too kind, too *servile*, too altruistic.

Later, when he was adult, he wondered if other cultures were also so *emotionally incestuous* as his own culture? And he found that tribal cultures, in their natural wisdom, know the pitfalls of the mother-son relation and thus build a strong father image and initiation rites—which serve precisely to liberate the male's sociability. Because otherwise it gets drowned in Gaia. Within these cultures, taboos such as the incest taboo, as well as taboos that concern the world of spirits are do-taboos. They are not talk-taboos. What is prohibited by the taboo is the deed, not the verbal expression of the tabooed behavior. In addition, these cultures organize festivities set out to *humanize* the taboo through its verbalization.

Language humanizes the taboo and integrates it into the individual and the collective unconscious.

He knew that if he had, even once, been able to *talk about all this with her*, it would have greatly alleviated the guilt-and-shame complex he was suffering from.

Spirituality is first of all the capability to *humanize asocial desires* through verbalization and, by doing this, to create culture. However, a speech taboo, a *non-dit* will not preserve culture, but destroy it; the tabooed behavior can't be comprehended as long as it is not *humanized by language*. It was such an odd thing. The communication would have had to be initiated by *her*. She was the adult—or supposed to be. But she had remained infantile, psychotic, fusioned with her own mother, idealizing her father.

She had not made the *genital transition* and remained on the stage of early, and archaic, anal homosexuality.

Speech taboos are the result of *hypocrisy* and serve to undermine the taboo since what is not talked about is done secretly while it is denunciated publicly. Language taboos are thus against democracy since democracy implies free speech.

He felt he was a slave and that democracy was something for grown-ups, that children had no rights. He was beaten in school. He was forced to eat what he had vomited. He had to stand in the corner, naked, at night, in the cold kitchen, for punishment, because he wanted to talk with his friend before falling asleep. The two female school principles ran to their Holy Church three times a day. They were obsessed with Church, with their Jesus, the Savior, with their *Gee Oh Dee*, their fucker. They had lost their husbands in the great war.

He knew, even as a child, that language education and the support of the young to express their emotions, thoughts and desires is overwhelmingly important for the formation and preservation of culture. Never heard of it. The fuck with intelligent children. They are *streamlined*. The drama of the gifted child is that he will become, and remain, a *Mute Hero*.

After the end of the Hellenic era and the beginning of the moralistic epoch of mankind (Nietzsche), and under the influence of post-platonic and Christian thought, language was more and more tabooed and the possibility of complete dialogue more and more narrowed.

Upon entering university, he was studying psychology. He found the books of *Robert M. Stein.* Psychotherapist Robert M. Stein calls the Judeo-Christian tradition primitive for this same reason. He says:

> ROBERT M. STEIN
>
> Creative psychological development, individuation, is dependent on spiritual freedom. When we say, for example, a man has a free spirit, do we mean that he freely or necessarily transgresses the imposed manners, mores and taboos of his culture? I think not. But it does mean the freedom to do anything or go any place he desires in the imaginal realm. He is a man who has clearly distinguished the sacral, timeless world from the secular, historical world. He knows he can move with unashamed dignity among the gods and demons which belong to the mundane world. Such freedom cannot occur with a primitive form of consciousness in which inner

and outer reality are governed by the same laws and values. In this sense, our Judeo-Christian tradition is primitive in that our thoughts and desires are subject to the same dogma, the same regulation, as our deeds. Spiritual freedom requires a break with biblical tradition and the development of a new form of consciousness – a consciousness which promotes the cultivation of imaginal freedom.

—Robert M. Stein, Redeeming the Inner Child in Marriage and Therapy, in: Reclaiming the Inner Child, ed. by Jeremiah Abrams, New York: Tarcher & Putnam, 1990, 261, 265.

He began to understand that cultures that prohibit language, such as ours, are in reality *no-cultures*. They are in their very root against freedom and against culture. They are barbarous, authoritarian and tyrannical. And their *'democratic setup'* and constitutions are blind man's buff.

The way to personal freedom and creativity, autonomy and the detachment from collective standard schemes of living is only possible through *individually* building a culture of language, through the personal, and admittedly *heroic* civilization of personal expression.

He built it through building his language, forging his vocabulary, expressing his thoughts, and setting up a *media galaxy* online. He knew that only on this very personal and individual basis true culture can be created for the community. For language is *all kinds of expression*, everything a creative mind may come up with, not only speech and writing, but also art, music and any nonverbal forms of utterance that lead to the sharing of ideas, concepts, visions, desires and emotions.

His worldview was the over-arching vision of a Renaissance genius. And like *Leonardo*, he was contemptuous, and eternally *disobedient*—as a lifestyle, so to say. He felt that every individual must *humanize their asocial instincts* through language.

He was aware that without language the *sublimation of the instincts* is impossible. In case that a given society lacks language to sublimate and transform asocial behavior, repression takes place. What is not integrated, is disintegrated, repressed and projected.

He studied history and saw that all collective tragedies of humanity, all wars and civil wars, genocide, massacres and holocausts were and are accompanied by *collective psychosis*, an explosion of irrational thought breaking through the fragile veil of life-denial, to bring to the surface the repressed desires in demonic amplification and distortion, and so to say, as collective forms of *perversion*. And he also found that it is the same on the individual level. An ego without language is a *psychotic* ego. Just as his mom was psychotic as her language had been impaired with stereotypes, and filled up with cultural garbage. He saw that the more her diction was spoiled and sullied, she fused and bonded with the mass and master mind, *newspaper-addicted, television-addicted, gossip-believer* and shallow soul. She who had been the *prototype of a critical mind,* antifascist, journalist and book author was reducing herself to a passive media consumer, thereby sealing her intellectual death!

And observing the decay of his mother, he sadly became aware that mute and speechless culture systematically breeds psychotic egos, and chaotic souls, and thus creates collective muteness that ultimately results in collective psychosis.

When he got his law diploma, he was depressed. She had wanted him to become a lawyer. *To Become.* While he had wanted *To Be.* And play. Be with children, to share *Life*, as a music teacher and pianist. An artist.

He thought, then, all went wrong. And he set out to study the *Tao.* The Tao of psychic health, he found, is *language*, communication, and the active use of spoken and written word.

To bring this about, it is not enough to write well-sounding guarantees in national constitutions and otherwise shut up.

He was different. He became a writer.

Sex and Reality

Civilization is talking almost always about *what is not essential.* And what civilization talks it creates. We live but the reality of our words and thoughts. There is no other.

When what is essential is taboo we create a split consciousness, a black-and-white picture where the missing gray shades represent the shades of truth we have discarded out of our daily perception.

A true culture *talks all* and therefore can restrain violent impulsive action. A false culture splits life off in 'good' and 'bad' and talks the good part in the office and the bad part in the brothel. This latter culture is ours. It *breeds violence* because what is not talked by the mouth is talked by the fist, and the gun. Sex talk is essential because it conveys essential content of living. *Sex is more important than shopping and home video.* With sex it's exactly as it is with health, as sex is not all the fun but without sex all is no fun.

Governments that try to suppress prostitution are *undermining the foundation of culture* and starve their people with the worst hunger there is, the hunger to penetrate and be penetrated. Sex is not just a pleasure function as sexologists explain to us. It's not just the orgasm, having orgasms repeatedly, daily, weekly or hourly.

Sex involves desires that are on a deeper level, such as *cannibalistic desires* and the desire for fusion with another. These desires, as they are not acted out in a civilized community, are *sublimated* in a wonderful way in sex and acted out, not *in realiter*, but on the unconscious level, during sexual activity and orgasm. Among these desires, the longing for active and passive penetration is perhaps the most important. And it's always, when we talk about desires, that nature has created the double-pair. There is no *yang* without *yin*.

By the same token, there is no wish to penetrate without a corresponding wish to be penetrated. There is no man to desire a girl-child without a girl-child desiring a man. There is no man wanting to penetrate a child without a child wanting to be penetrated by a man. All rhetoric denying this simple fact of nature serves purposes not related to sex, *economic interests* first of all. Those who defy natural love must fill that vacuum in some way; *materialistic consumer culture has grown as a result of this vacuum* and it attempts to fill the gap.

The child that is not sperm-nourished eats ice cream, *needs* ice cream. *Nicecream.* Hence, what naturally is free becomes, with a certain alienated logic, a *consumer good*, and people ram into their minds the needs their mother-society thus artificially creates by distorting nature.

The Porno Hero

Most of us have forgotten that our bodies were the first and certainly the most natural source of pleasure. He knew it from his most tender years. He had been *awake*. He had been conscious. *His life was lust*. He saw that most people lived lives not their own.

Alienated from their bodies, they seemed to compensate for the lost-paradise-of-being through *having*, possessing, consuming. He observed that the things they are attached to give them a glimpse of the joy they could have if they kept true to what is laid in their cradle.

Their dilemma starts in early childhood. The progress of civilization seems to have a heavy price. We pay for it with our bodies that we gradually destroy. For a body that is not connected to a soul is a *dead body*. The process of alienation that leads to this gradual decay of the human body is an integral part of the conditioning for consumer society. It begins as early as in childhood.

He observed it in boarding school. There were the *lovers* and the *fuckers*. The *lovers*, that was the small group that he himself belonged to, the minority. They came back from the weekend at Sunday night, and would have sex until way after midnight, and the boarding turned into a brothel where boy desired boy.

And they were tender, gentle, intelligent. Often, after sex, they would talk to each other, for hours, whispering from one bed to the other, in the huge cold dormitory. And the *fuckers* arrived arrogantly Monday morning, with their fat parents, in their fat cars. Their parents were butchers, doctors and lawyers, established, and *straight*. And their sons were fuckers, of that sort that is now the prevailing vintage of imbecility on this globe. Means they did not fuck. Their *fuck was stuck*, and that is why they turned foul, perverse, violent, persecutory, mean, stupid, and dominant. They were the *consumers*.

He saw that porno was a form of consumption. *Consuming a body.* As a lifestyle.

Modern society is organized that way, he knew as a child. He understood it might be profitable. People wanna fuck. Children wanna play. So the fuckers buy toys and give them to their children. The toy industry sustains the entire structure of the consumer society. Without the early conditioning toward toys as a body pleasure ersatz, people would not accept the later *ersatz satisfactions* they receive for the sacrifice of primary body pleasure.

What is primary body pleasure? he wondered. It is the pleasure that already the small child derives from playing with the body.

—And yet, he lectured in the boarding, at night, with his friends as an attentively listening audience, we are afraid to do it, right? And why are we afraid? It's *our* body, no? It's not the body of our parents, of our teachers. *It's ours.* And yet we are afraid. So *something must be wrong,* either with us or with this fuck society. Whereupon they called him *sex professor,* because of his early discourses on the nature of sex and the mechanisms of sordid manipulation children are subjected to in this pigstall of a culture.

Pleasure is essentially sexual pleasure. The moral and societal prohibition of child sexuality is the *condition* for the functioning of a civilization patterned upon *ersatz* satisfactions. This fact, that he understood as early as in childhood, makes intelligible the research results that observe a *direct correlation* between the civilization standard of any given society and the severity of its child sex taboo.

As a young student, then, he studied Freud who thought man develops creativity through the *sublimation* of his primary sexual desire. Culture is thought to be the product of a *transformation of original libido into a form of creative energy* that serves cultural purposes.

Is this thesis true? he wondered.

Upon further inquiry, he found that it is *true and not true* at the same time. It is true insofar as the transformation of desire leads in fact to a form of culture, *an ersatz for the original culture* that would have been created through living our original instincts. And he found that it is not true in the sense that sublimation leads to an *ersatz culture* and not a true and original culture. That is why he came to believe that our culture is not a culture, but a non-culture, because it is an *ersatz* culture.

Whereupon he looked at ancient cultures, for example at the Cretan culture that did not repress sexual pleasure, neither in children nor in adults; and he saw how high human civilization can grow on the basis not of sublimation but of *real satisfaction* of sexual desires of all kinds. He became more and more convinced that in many ways Cretan culture had been superior to our modern culture, more developed, more knowledgeable and, last not least, more *peaceful and harmonious*. He was depressed to learn about the sudden and brutal end of this immensely creative culture through the invasion of Barbarian patriarchal tribes. He found that that was one of the turning points in human history. Turning points for culture to turn into *pig culture*. It was from this time and parallel events in other cultures that humanity took the turn into *pseudo-culture*, that the artificial and hypocrite, the stupid and doctrinaire, the false and arrogant, together with *violence, war and destruction* began to dominate the natural and *naturally intelligent* original cultures that preceded them.

He saw that all leading religions absolved and baptized this turn of humanity into the false, manipulative and undemocratic *Barbarian Primal Horde* that represents present-day mainstream culture. They have consciously played the role of a *catalyzer* in the conditioning of man for war and destruction – although they globally pay lip service to the contrary.

When he was at the height of his new career, as a corporate trainer and human resource expert, he began to study the culture and lifestyle of tribal peoples, admiring their wistful ways to realize human potential, and their unique manners of helping children learn about themselves, acquiring self-knowledge from their most tender years.

It is significant that tribal cultures who put the human body and *body sensitivity* in the foreground of cultural, artistic and social life do not need to preach love. *They love.* And they do not need to heal love because they *practice love.* Their religion is not the integrity of pseudo-moralistic values, but the integrity of *love.* He knew he had found his Grail.

Religion, in tribal cultures, is not a power factor and does not exert power over individuals, he found. They practice the *true religio*, giving guidance to people in search for truth about coming and going, transcendence of suffering, care for the sick and the needy, for those who acted against the law, and the dying. He came to admire the *North American Indians* for having preserved forms of this original and pure religion that was once universal for all human beings and that originated in Hawaii, as *Huna*, practiced by the *Kahunas*, natives of that island.

As a child, he was a pornographer. He loved what is obscene and found the obscene in art. He loved art in its innocent joy for exhibiting the obscene and grotesque in human behavior that is motivated by the desire to break through the reigning structures of pleasure denial and to propagate a sort of *revolution of pleasure*. He found he was born into a stupid, dull murder culture that had no idea of helping the young to unfold their unique potential. He felt neglected as a child, as a youngster. He was utterly lonely. He was the *Porno Hero* for in porno he found a companion. He saw that obscenity is not focused on beauty, but on ugliness. He became aware that pornography is often not interested in the beautiful and aesthetic in human nature, but in what is vulgar and hideous.

However, he began to doubt if this is a general characteristic of pornography or if pornography in the repressive culture, in its anti-ism, has twisted human nature? He was at pains to give a definitive answer to the question as he missed empirical data regarding the *function of pornography* in cultures lesser repressive than ours. He had a look at societies that are completely sexually permissive, such as the *Trobriand* culture of Papua New-Guinea, and he noted that there was no pornography at all to find in such cultures!

This was how he came to believe that the need for pornography is a *product of repression itself,* and not a fanciful turn of the human sexual drive. And he found *affirmative evidence* for the fact that pornography is molded from the negative of the society where it is to be found, not from the positive.

While it is deformed creativity, it is creativity nonetheless!

And yet it doesn't oppose the values of the society that has produced it, but unconsciously identifies with them. He then began to understand the logic of pornography. Hence, a violent society will produce violent porno. A society that does not love children will exhibit children as sex objects and consumable sweets, fuck puppets for sale, for daily use and abuse.

Then he studied people who produce pornography—the so-called pornographers. He saw that they have been conditioned to the false values of the society they have grown up in, even though they may not live by these values.

He came to see that the fantasies that are at the basis of their productions were themselves being created by social inhibitions and taboos, on one hand, and individual traumatic experiences, on the other.

However, he found that this was true for all art.He was an artist, first of all. He became aware that the pleasure in obscenity is not limited to pornography.

He saw that the taste for the obscene is to be found massively in modern art and that it has strong roots in antiquity. And that it had a great comeback in surrealism.

Dali would be *unthinkable* without obscenity that is, in his art, directly linked to the scurrilous, mystic and humoristic-sarcastic.

When he studied the art of Andy Warhol, and especially his early obscene films, he found that it can be the goal of a pornographic artist to exhibit the emotional and sexual exploitation of women and children through the pornographic exhibition of *rape*.

But he reasoned that it is also possible to achieve this same goal by showing what officially is precluded in our society, *consenting* sexual relationships between adults and children.

He met a paradox. Strangely enough, he thought to himself, in the first case one would not talk about pornography, although degrading sexual acts would be shown, whereas in the second case, even though no violence had been exhibited, most people would judge such material as being *pornographic.*

What is it that makes the difference in this strange value judgment? It seems that it is the fact that in the first case the motivation of the author was to talk about *violence* whereas in the second case the intention of the author was to show possible unconventional forms of *pleasure.* It is only logical that a violence-based society finds violence more acceptable than pleasure. A pleasure-based society will logically find violence pornographic.

When he worked with children, he saw that little children *do not know these value judgments,* and that freely raised children, while they may exhibit pornographic interests or behavior, display such behavior only for short interludes. He found that children love the outlandish, the scurrilous, the macabre and the unusual, and the obscene. In all they do, he observed, children are primarily pleasure-oriented. But since they have subtle antennas for the tolerance level of their adult environment, they quickly adapt to those values, simply for avoiding the *displeasure resulting from punishment and reject* for non-accepted forms of conduct.

He found that this was the sole reason why obscenity was so difficult to observe in children. The observer needs to enjoy their full trust and they themselves must grow up in a basically free and nonviolent milieu. Only if these conditions are met, he found, there is a chance *that they dare to openly admit or exhibit* their obscene wishes and desires.

He then asked the question when, and under which conditions an obscene production can be considered as *art?* He found that this depends on the *intention of the author*. A film can for example serve to demonstrate a certain situation or event. In this case we would qualify it as a reportage. Even though it may exhibit obscene, pornographic or even revolting facts, it would not generally be considered as a pornographic production. A pornographic production is primarily oriented at exhibiting obscene events or acts and is guided by a *commercial interest*, and this is the criterion that shows a production is not art, but pornography. It's the commercial expectation. He then again looked at Warhol and found that to judge Warhol's early films as pornographic obviously shuns and overlooks the artistic intention of the author which was at the basis of their production. Thus, he reasoned, the difference consists in the sole fact that a production is *intended to be art*, or else is intended to make money, entertain, show off, etc. Today, *art and sexuality* is a recurring theme in every museum exhibition agenda. The artistic intention in most of the art that exhibits nudity or sexual encounters is *oriented toward the ideal of human beauty* or the beauty of the human body or else the beauty of the human embrace as a *form of communication.* (Actually the word *fornication* comes closest to convey that *all sexual intercourse is communication,* as all social intercourse is communication). But it can also be focused upon ugliness or vulgarity. It seems that for most erotic artists the exhibition of the human beauty is their *primary aesthetic ideal.*

After studying Warhol's early cinema and art, he became interested in photography, and he came to admire the art of Lewis Carroll and David Hamilton. If we take, for example, the girl photographs of Lewis Carroll and

David Hamilton, we can make out ideals that these photographers subscribe to: an *aesthetic ideal* and a *sexual ideal*. With Carroll, the sexual ideal may be twisted into abstinence from desire, but even though this ideal is negative, it is still present. In fact, in their white-collared *purity*, these girls are highly erotic. With Hamilton, he found, there is less of a doubt that the erotic ideal is related to the beauty and the charm of young girls, even though typically in Hamilton's photography the girls do definitely not look sexy but in the contrary rather apathetic and disinterested. He guessed that this was intentional and served the other, aesthetic, ideal in Hamilton's photography which is primarily a *poetic* ideal.

Thus, he came to acknowledge that both photographers share this ideal of creating, through their art, a *poetic reality*.

On the other hand, he contemplated the productions of the highly successful child photographer Kim Anderson. Anderson's children portraits that today are to be found at virtually every kiosk and on calendars, post cards, carnets, book covers and alike in every stationary store, are highly unreal, if not artificial.

The purity that irradiates from those children is one that has no parallel in real life. The children are depicted as objects, furniture, degraded to *kitsch*. The photos themselves, it is true, are professional arrangements, most of them a combination of b/w photography and coloring of the negatives done by hand, as a post-production artwork. And the sublime sense of color of the artist is unique. He acknowledged the mastery behind this highly aesthetic photography. And yet, he found that the child as a person was non-existing in this photography which may suggest the conclusion that this photography is but another form of obscenity.

The exhibition of children as mere puppets and pleasure dolls has a long tradition. Carroll broke with this tradition.

Alice Liddell is truly alive on those photos, and she is still today. However, what is popular today is not Carroll, but Anderson, not the child as a person, but the child as a projection object, a fetish for a world of adults who have lost their inner child. Anderson's children photos are indeed representative for a culture that denies the child to have a body and a right to decide about this body. And this is probably the reason why she became world-famous.

It's easy to be successful when one swings with one's cultural bias and affirms it scientifically, poetically or artistically.

SEX AND SOUL

The reason why most of us are so screwed up is accumulated tension because of lacking fuck when we were small. We know that.

You know it. I know it. But *we do as if we did not know it* and continue our boring hamburger lives that lack not only the soul of meaning, but also the soul of sex.

Sex, we have, and everywhere. But where is the *soul* of it? Forgotten, lost, considered as *kitsch*, a yellowish photo from olden times when men wore long hair and had *good manners* when they greeted a little girl. Home theater with Lewis Carroll and Alice Liddell as haunting spirits. Sunday at Grandma's, and the children nervous and restless, and when the milk turned sour, they were sodomized, one by one. A fat-assed dummy with horny loins sprouted up from the cellar like an unwanted wine.

Some of the more intelligent girls appreciated the ritual-like fashion of that rather brutish game, while the boys just surrendered like obedient soldiers in the Turkish army when the hack order was the distilled version of the fuck order.

Sex without soul is like hastily chewing a hamburger at a table without cover and napkin, and drinking the beer from the bottle as if it was baby's first milk.

Sex without soul is what we have today in the West, and from there spreading worldwide, and that is sex without emotion, *cool* sex. It fits very well in our other cool *softdrink and handphone values*, our other cool handshakes, our other cool party achievements.

Puritans are afraid that childlovers bring in *hot, emotional and soulful sex* through the backdoor of Anaïs Nin's *House of Incest*, and that even the most active and obsessed churchgoer will be turned into a *hard-on child-fucking devil*—when stores are closed and doors are locked. Those that are eternally worried about right-and-wrong-sex should worry more about *soul*.

In decades of church-running they never learnt that you have to run nowhere to be connected with all-that-is, the real *Cosmic Internet,* the total non-virtual reality.

THE NEUROTIC HERO

Modern child psychology is truly a master science. Not only because it works masterly with public relations, and in some way is but a branch of it, but because it serves the *masters*.

And the *Neurotic Hero*, who represented the masters in the *Committee of Child Protectors*, proudly announced: *We are going to produce the clean and sexless child because that's what our industry needs*. The masters who have many names, agreed.

The slave who has only one name, *child*, was not asked. The child is pampered and over-protected until showing all the signs that are desirable in child slavery. Thus the sexually disabled slave child will show the following four characteristics: fear, foul, false, fake.

Fortissimo. The *Neurotic Hero* is born. Let me explain.

Fear. When bioenergy is repressed, the pent-up vital energy produces inner tension and strife that we experience as an undesirable heat-flow that is typically accompanied by a blockage in the solar plexus together with heart palpitations: we call this *fear*. It is simply a matter of *body energetics* that the sexually repressed child becomes anxious, fearful and murky.

Foul. At the same time, the open-hearted refreshing attitude that we know from sexually active children becomes *foul*.

The fear-complex renders the child coward and numb, and introvert, which manifests in a characterological *foulness*. The child's face begins to look *dirty* or *murky* instead of showing the typical *sparkling* and *fresh* complexion of the emotionally sane and active child. This foulness is essentially the result of the mix between anxiety and guilt.

False. The anxious, coward and murky-looking child becomes deeply *false.* They begin to *lie,* even to a point that they do not know anymore what's true and what's false, and thus develop a *fantasy* character. These are the kids that tell parents, friends or police any story and, incredibly so, are generally taken for *truthful and credible.*

Fake. The false child that has developed all the characteristics to survive in a culture that denies them the free expression of emotions and sexual feelings begins to crave for *pleasure compensation* in the form of *fake:* plastic toys, coke, hamburgers, junk food, *fashion* clothes and stink shoes exclusively from *big brands.* Ultimately, the child becomes what it craves for, fake. A fake being in a fake culture.

The *Neurotic Hero*, prototype of the 21st century human in postmodern industrial culture will be the *ultimate killer app* for the rest of humanity.

Let them grow up and then we talk again—if we get the *chance!*

HOT AND SWEATY

What about our hot-and-sweaty endeavors? Put them on ice? *Leads to ice-cold violence.* Repress them? *Leads to cancer.* Forget about them? *Leads to Alzheimer.* Make them down? *Leads to prison.* Get them in business? *Leads to little girls …*

As a little boy I was really thinking that adults who are well off and decent had no sexual desires. I thought that only the mean and vulgar ones were engaging in something we boys were addicted to. It's perverse to be addicted to what at the same time you are making down as bad, vulgar, dirty and shameful. While it is healthy to be addicted to something you really *value.*

When you are convinced that sex is good and brings joy, laughter and relaxed and funny moments to people, then you may well be addicted to it. *This addiction, then, does not hurt you.*

He went on and on studying classical piano, playing it, or trying to, and experienced only frustration. Over many years. Simply because, within the *realm of classical music,* what is worthwhile to be played is too difficult to play. And what is easy to play is not worth the effort to be studied. Because it is petty stuff. Invariably, the music where the composer put his heart and soul, and his *genius* is difficult and complex. It is not an easy tune for brain-cut school girls who hammer down everything that comes under their dirty fingers. And most what is sold as piano exercises is not worth the paper it is printed upon. And even when you get one level up and play Brahms' piano etudes, *you certainly do valuable training, however only for playing Brahms*, and not for playing Bach, Chopin or Rachmaninov.

And in general I would rather follow Svjatoslav Richter's advice and play Brahms right away instead of *preparing for playing* Brahms. The first mode is the *real one*, the second mode is the *virtual one*. The first mode leads to play Brahms, *recht und schlecht*, whereas the second mode *buries your creativity before you ever got off the ground* because you are never going to play Brahms.

It is part and parcel of our civilization to appreciate only what is painful and belittle what comes easily and without effort. That is why *Superlearning* remains an esoteric and high-priced language learning technique for diplomats and top-managers while it was originally developed as a method for bringing out the most in the child in Kindergarten.

In fact, Georgi Lozanov, a brilliant psychoanalyst from Bulgaria, had researched the way *we learn our mother tongue* when we are still in babyhood. And he found that the brain picks up and stores away *whole patterns* including the grammar which explains why most of us speak only one language perfectly and without accent, the one we learnt in early childhood.

THE STUPID HERO

The *Stupid Hero* was born in school. Historically, stupidity was the result of introducing children to the school system.

What is school? A special vintage of prison. Created by the Church. For what purpose? For creating the *Stupid Hero*.

Why and how did schools come up? When, in the dark age, the Church tried to gain as much power over people as possible and indulged in abuses of all kinds, monks and nuns opened the first schools.

These schools were recruitment centers for the monasteries. From the beginning, boys and girls were separated. Why?

Sex is in the way when it goes to create the *Stupid Hero*. It makes people intelligent, that's why sex is on the index in all right-wing fascist societies. From the boys' classes, the monks were recruited, from the girls' schools the nuns.

Schools were destined to assuring the Church gets well-trained functionaries. They needed *Stupid Heroes*. Guess why.

Of course, when you read history books, the Church is painted as the great benefactor of humanity in implementing the school system. But in reality the Church's intention was first of all an effort to sustain the power of its own worldly hierarchy and highly effective oppression system, and second, and most importantly, *direct perception of truth* was going to be wiped out from civilization from that point in history.

Before the existence of schools, children were raised by nature and preserved their natural intelligence. They were at home, close to their parents and the other adults present in the extended family. They learned primarily by observation and *direct perception*. They *picked up* what they needed for their later career, from their early environment. It is interesting to remember, in this context, that early language learning takes place in exactly the same way. *The young child picks up whole patterns from the language spoken around him or her.*

The *Stupid Hero* unlearnt all this in school.

New research in recent years made clear that this kind of learning is much more holistic and adapted to the passively organizing intelligence of the human brain than any system that has so far been implemented in schools. Therefore human beings generally learn their first language, or mother tongue, perfectly, whereas they cripple along, as *Stupid Heroes*, learning a second or third language later in school or at college.

Only relatively recent learning methods such as Dr. Lozanov's *Superlearning* have taken serious the wisdom of nature as it is present in every early learning experience. Think tanks such as Edward de Bono have in addition shown us the relevance of the brain's functioning as a *passively self-organizing system*. Edward de Bono found that our learning curricula in schools, universities or, more specifically, in *management training*, are awkwardly maladapted to the way our brain organizes and stores information. De Bono, much in the same way as Dr. Lozanov, found that only in early childhood learning, and especially in the way young children learn their first language, we see nature's full intelligence at work.

It is a well-known fact that geniuses such as Albert Einstein, Pablo Picasso and many others among our wonderful creators never finished school, dropped out or flew it. They knew that they knew better and followed their instinct rather than an artificial method that represents an enormous waste of time and resources and which violates human dignity in the most flagrant way.

Life, seen through the eyes of a school system, is but a mechanistic, dead system that, pretty much in the style of the vivisectionists, has to be killed in order to be ready for study.

Methods like *Superlearning* start from the insight that we have to involve the parts of the brain that have been left out by evolution in order to activate man's highest learning potential. In fact, modern man who deems himself so advanced in knowledge and wisdom uses only five to eight percent of his potential. What then is evolution all about? Looking back in history and becoming aware of the high degree of wisdom that man possessed in ancient times, we cannot seriously pretend that there was evolution *at all*. In the contrary, man has deteriorated during the process of what we use to call *civilization*.

We must head into developing the *right brain hemisphere* and the *brain stem*. It will begin with *learning how to learn*, with unblocking our potential for true receptiveness, for whole-brain learning, for using our brain for what it is destined for: learning by absorbing *whole patterns* instead of isolated pieces of knowledge. It will begin with *holistic education*, and it will be electronic learning. And eventually it will pass into the school and schooling systems worldwide.

As long as we continue to bring up and being brought up in idiotic systems that flagrantly violate our true intelligence, we will breed but confusion and violence. There is no question that, then, we will not be able to master the challenges of the new era we are heading into: the *Information Age*, the *New Age*, the *Aquarius Age*. Only through holistic solutions that involve our wholeness and the integration of all parts of our being will we be able to survive in the mess that we ourselves, or our past generations, have bread.

Learning through *direct perception* is the way out, and it is actually a way back; back to intelligence and to the teachings of the ancient mystery schools where perennial wisdom was once taught to an elite.

But I know that *you* prefer to remain a *Stupid Hero.*

THE CHILD HERO

Another hero that is worshipped in postmodern international consumer culture is the *child hero.*

The child hero is the prototype of the consumer child, bravely compliant with their own braincut, their own emotional and sexual mutilation and left-brain hypertrophy, their own *implosion* leading to their later selection as best-of-best among *Stupid Heroes.*

The child hero pervades the toy and video game industry. It has become institutionalized as the *child role model* for the consumer child in Oedipal culture. It's the ever-smiling toy companion, the Peter Pan leader in a fairy world of gnomes that will eternally remain gnomes. *Wanna grow up, lil' one? No, brotha, I'm so well off here, so well protected, so well cared for! How can I ever live in that brutal world out there? I think I not wanna grow up. Never ever. Period.*

So they become *peer leaders in the fairy world of modern childhood*, little brave robots who explain the why's and how's of all prohibitions, so sagely admonished by the grown-ups, with the *child's best* in mind. So they come to teach the values and the rules of the game of child repression, through their millions of copies of so-called educational games spammed and sported, sold and exported all over the world by the *big leaders*, the grown up role models.

Society has eventually *grown up*. The modern mainstream parent does not need brutality anymore to transform a sane lively child into a hyper-active, insomniac and emotionally starved consumer child. He's got a better toolset, and a more cunning strategy.

Use the peer set of values and little brave robots that are well designed, well groomed and well educated, that bring over the messages, and directly into the unconscious of our little fellows. Effective education, effective programming, effective results.

Information has a place. In the *children's room* first of all. It's for little people who are able to know truth to effectively prevent them from using that ability, and as early as possible.

They need to live with, and be continually fed with, consumer society's many myths and fairy tales. These myths are the *fuel* of million people's lives.

And these millions are deeply moved not by children, but by football.

THE FOOTBALL HERO

No hero culture can do without football. From my earliest childhood I remember to have hated football. As television was not yet available when I was a small child, I got to know about football when I entered boarding school.

And there and then I was beaten up because I preferred piano playing over football. The footballers were the majority. They were the fuckers.

It was the same in school. The *natural sciences* were representing the strong majority values and art and music the queer and *random* subject matters. Of course, in a society of imbecile *football worshippers*, philosophers, musicians and artists are considered as subversive rats.

And by the same token, in the world of Football Heroes, *muscle* is the order of the day. I would agree if it was *one* day. But now I'm forty years older and *nothing* has changed in this situation since the days of my childhood. So, I'm slightly fed up. Else, I'm *bored*. That's why I avoid this whole society and live my own life.

I thought I was born in a *change generation* but I honestly ask: where is the change? It got better and then it got worse.

It got away from football and into free sex and joyful love relations with children, only to switch back even more violently into repression and fascism.

And from regional and national football, we got into the *international football religion* as part of postmodern consumer culture. On my recent trip to Lima, Peru, I was requesting to eat a pizza unfootballed, but that was proving to be an *impossible quest*. Virtually no restaurant was to be found in *Miraflores*, a nice residential quarter of Lima, to have a quiet dinner. Football is not a game, it's a religion, an ideology.

To contradict football makes your life messy and nobody will trust you. It's just as contradicting the importance of *McDonalds* or *Coca Cola*, and not for nothing these and other multinationals are so fervently copulating with footballers all over the world. Everything sells better when it's sold through the name of a famous footballer.

Psychoanalyzing the football religion, it's clear that it is based on sex repression, male dominance, barking arrogance and a *compensation for sex* in the form of a game where a ball-penis has to be put in a goal-vagina, whereby '*running, passing or kicking*' (Webster Dictionary). What I saw in

Peru and other countries in Latin America, the Caribbean, the United States and European countries is that football serves a function in *sex-repressive education*. It has for this purpose been used ever since, in so-called *religious institutions*, for educating orphans and keeping them away from having sex with each other. It serves as well in public education.

And from what I saw in South America, football is actively used for *re-conditioning* street children to the values of global consumer culture in all the homes for street children I have visited in Brazil, Peru and Ecuador. The male directors of these homes left no doubt that street children used sex as a *drug* against depression. The teachers were for this reason rather positive regarding child-child sex games as they compared the *sex drug* with the drugs of gasoline sniffing or crack and had to admit that the *natural drug of sex* did not cause the damage those synthetic industrial drugs were causing in the minds and bodies of children. And yet, as they were working for the Church, they more or less had to accept the *brainwashing* paradigm and while the street children I encountered in the street where lively, happy, joyful and full of energy, those I encountered in Church organizations, those *saved ones*, so to say, were true caricatures of their street counterparts: unhappy, infantilized, depressed, dependent, and craving for affection.

When they wanted a hug from a worker, they were smilingly told to join the afternoon football match! When they wanted to have sex in the dormitory, they were told by a child psychologist at bed time that sex was *okay* except *abusing other kids* at night, and other niceties of the same sort.

It's as if you say to a child who has got only a red trousers *Well, yes, it's permitted to wear trousers in our home, except red ones.* I am quite sure that their forced drug regimen change from gasoline or crack to industrially produced *medical* tranquillizers and anti-depressants will get these kids to the moon within a few years. And then they can happily close the file cabinet. Problem solved. *Forever.* And this will, then, be the ultimate sacrifice for *Jesus Christ Our Savior* they are supposed to give for having been *saved* in *His* name. These children will thus incarnate the ultimate heroes of postmodern international consumer culture.

They will have enriched pharmaceutical multinationals and that's why they will ultimately be *blessed* – with a last will for their last supper. *God Bless the Child*, the *dead* child. It will humbly not cause further expenditure and nourish the earth with its flesh and soul.

Holy football serves many goals, not only sex repression. It serves most vital materialistic goals. It makes money rolling cross-culturally and, yes, *legally*, while the same is true for drug dealing. But the latter must be done underground since it's considered as *bad*. And clearly, somebody who smokes a joint will hardly engage in a game where he's got kicked in all possible ways just for *fucking* a *fucking* ball into a *fucking* net.

And when I extrapolate these insights into a more philosophical sphere, I must admit that *playing the game* is not for me and was not since school times.

My parents had enough latitude, despite the many problems they were struggling with, to raise me *unfootballed and unconditioned for a large part* and that is why they are in my loving memories for all times! They themselves were not *playing the game* during Hitlerism in Germany, and that game was surely harder and a hell more fucking than football. It was a game for life and death because if you didn't want to join the NSDAP you got to have no doctorate or if you didn't want to betray and kill *Systemfeinde*, you had to be shot dead. Both of them escaped as they must have been protected by their guardian angels, but their psychic and emotional suffering was such that they were *broken* as humans for the rest of their lives. And yet for me they were and are *heroes, the true heroes there are in this broken world*, not those fake-heroes that are famous in postmodern culture. Thus I had the privilege already as a small child to go unconditioned and nobody forced me to subscribe to the *football values* that I saw were pervading most of my school and university colleagues. And this ultimately allowed me to question the *football religion* and see what is behind it, while I observe that most of my fellows are unable to get there.

Yin Power

Yin and yang are complementary forces, not opposites. Yet it is a challenge to represent and incarnate *yin* values in a culture that depreciates them. The art of living is to dare *a step further than the atrophied intelligence of mass culture* seems to allow: it's to realize the *yin-yang balance* on the individual level.

How is it possible to live with a *balanced yin-yang relationship* in a culture that is so daringly unbalanced about it?

The art of living is a true art: nothing easy and nothing easy to achieve. Taoism and Buddhism both are offering ways to the lover of spirit, through daily ritual, refinement and self-development, that go beyond survival and teach the unique art of living a balanced life.

Taoism and Buddhism are beyond worship, and therefore are superior religions. They are offering ways to realize one's Way, one's *Tao*. They do not impose any specific Way, but teach, in an abstract and impersonal manner, the techniques and the spirit of bringing about the qualities of one's personal way of life.

In a society with a hypertrophied *yang*, to bring about a *yin-yang* balance on a personal level is only possible by emphasizing your *Yin Power*. Lao-tzu was the spiritual teacher of true *Yin Power* and as such a rare exception in a landscape of rigid machismo values that is the imbecile outcome of patriarchy. And therefore his teaching, such as Heraclites' in the West, never became a guiding rule for the a-cultural mob of modern society. But even among the educated classes of industrial cultures, the majority will follow a *rigid moralistic paradigm* rather than a naturally intelligent one: that is why in modern Chinese society Confucius is the guiding spirit, and not his god, Lao-tzu. And it is the same in the West. Intellectual values even today are founded upon the neurotic stupidities of Aristotle and not upon the truly intelligent *flow* philosophy that was taught by Heraclites.

Today, because of quantum science, a few initiated intellectuals in the West and East begin to understand what poets always knew: that what we need to study are the flow principles, not only in physics, but *in life.*

Whoever knows how nature flows, knows to flow himself and is able to lead a flexible and balanced life. Looking at a baby crawling over the floor teaches all about life. Or watching a tiger. Or a simple cat. To put your foot in a

manner that is totally balanced, totally
focused, totally natural. To put your foot in a
way like the wind blows: spontaneously. In a
way that is so trivial that it is the way of a
genius.

All genuinely lived lives seem to be trivial,
but actually are *extraordinarily complex* and
top-of-the-line. All genuinely natural lives are
aesthetic. Suffices to see a beautiful little girl,
a handsome little boy, walking up to you.
What is more natural grace, more
extraordinary charm, more spontaneous
intelligence than those present in healthy
lovely children? My piano style was strongly
influenced by both Keith Jarrett and Serge
Rachmaninov. Jarrett is not enough
Rachmaninov and Rachmaninov is not enough
Jarrett.

That is why I try to make the synthesis of
both. And please don't tell me that Jarrett was

not a composer but a pianist and Rachmaninov was not a pianist but a composer. Both views are wrong. Both men are both composers and pianists. Both men are geniuses.

Both men are enriching the human heart by an extraordinary impact that is not only musical, but also philosophical, not only pianistic but also spiritual.

THE COFFEE HERO

> Coffee has not been without its detractors, but they have always been in the minority. Coffee was widely blamed for the death of the French minister Colbert, who died of stomach cancer. Goethe blamed his habitual *caffè latte* for his chronic melancholia and his attacks of anxiety.
>
> – TERENCE MCKENNA, FOOD OF THE GODS, A RADICAL HISTORY OF PLANTS, DRUGS AND HUMAN EVOLUTION, LONDON: RIDER, 1992, P. 185 (CONTRA COFFEE).

The hero culture is a *coffee culture*.

From my earliest childhood I remember I preferred tea over coffee. This is quite interesting because I was born literally in coffee, so to say, as my mother gave me birth *at home* and that meant, in an extension of my parents' coffee shop.

Everything around there was related to coffee, the smell of the roasting coffee first of all, the sight of the huge copper roasting machine that turned all the time and that made an intriguing sound, almost like a song, the large sacks of raw coffee in the corners, the staples of old newspapers that served for wrapping the coffee sold to a client (at this time in post-war Germany there was not yet any plastic wrapping paper), and the brownish dust that covered just everything and that was an inevitable byproduct of the roasting process.

Then later, when I was an adolescent, just after entering boarding school, my mother received a brochure from *Paul Schrader, Tea and Coffee* from Bremen and first ordered some coffee there. Upon my initiative then she got to order tea as well, and that was really a discovery for both of us. Over the next months I could convince my mother that *tea was better than coffee*, and until her death, more than thirty years later, she almost exclusively drank tea. And that is kind of astonishing as she related to me that the time she was pregnant she drank around five liters of coffee per day. I said I was born in coffee, right … ?

For me, the shift was more dramatic. I did not touch coffee anymore while during my earlier childhood I had abused of it (as well as of all kinds of alcoholic beverage when I could get hold of it), and became a fervent tea drinker.

Every Sunday afternoon, my mother and me had our tea ritual, and when taking the train to the boarding school in the evening I usually did not sleep the whole night, and this for two reasons. Tea and sex.

With my mother we drank about ten to twenty cups of tea per day and so in the night I was alert like a mouse, and only after having had extensive sex with my favorite peer boy in the home, I could finally get to sleep in the early morning hours. And I began to like my life. While my earlier childhood was a dreadful experience as I was cruelly mistreated in a Catholic home, life in that boarding home was not bad as they even had a piano, school was interesting and challenging, and my friend Philippe was just the sweetest boy one can dream of. Still today I tend to think if the world was populated by men like Philippe, that would be a peaceful gorgeous world. I just loved him with all my heart, soul and body, and it was mutual. Our love was the best kept secret in the boarding school, to say that it was no secret at all and everybody laughed about it which sometimes was hard to bear for us.

Well, let me get one level deeper in my philosophical considerations of coffee, tea and sex. For me, today coffee is related to Christianity, left-brain upbringing, angst, prejudice, violence and Western culture; sexually it is related to what I call *fake heterosexuality*; tea for me today is related to Buddhism and Taoism, a balanced mind when both brain hemispheres work in synch, latitude and wisdom, peacefulness and Eastern culture; sexually it is related to *true heterosexuality* but also a complete openness toward any other nonviolent enjoyable sexual preference, such as *pedophilia*.

I was thinking on these lines since childhood and youth. I could never share these insights as I had hardly any words for them at the time.

I found my reasoning so utterly unusual that I was afraid friends would either laugh in my face or reject me, or both, when I voiced these thoughts.

Only after I found Terence McKenna's considerations about coffee related to Christian and Western culture in *Food of the Gods*, I woke up to my own insights and began to put them on paper. And there was the poetic dimension. I was very impressed by a poem written by Paul Celan, entitled *Die Todesfuge* that we read in German class at high school and that related coffee to concentration camps.

Schwarze Milch der Frühe, wir trinken dich abends, began that poem. Our teacher said this poem was one of Celan's best because of the mastery association between the black color of coffee, in concentration camps the only kind of *food* there was for weeks and weeks, and the metaphorical black color of angst and death. And I must think of all those *cowboy films* I saw in my childhood and John Wayne drinking coffee, except when he was busy kissing a woman or shooting a man down, or riding the horse. Yes, that was a *coffee ritual*, not just drinking coffee.

Often Wayne was sitting by a fire with that metal cup in his big hand and it seemed like he was *being friends* with coffee, that coffee really had an importance in his life, just like women and guns. And when I joined university and got a job in the law library I saw the huge importance coffee has at the workplace, especially in universities. It's more than a ritual. It's a religion. Christianity is a coffee religion. Both are black. Buddhism is a tea religion. Both are green.

And then the taste.

Coffee is bitter, obtrusive, narrow, anxiety-inducing, dull, and chasing your thought. It works pretty much like beer, putting you a headboard in front of your mind. Tea is subtle, with multiple fragrances, non-obtrusive, opening the latitude and wisdom of insight, taking a headboard off your mind, and clearing your thought.

It is obvious that coffee, in the way it works on the mind, is related to *mind-closing* drugs like alcohol and a fear-ridden, obsessive and highly regulated sexuality, while tea is related to *mind-opening* drugs such as plant entheogens and a fearless consenting and highly permissive self-regulated sexuality.

It's not for nothing that the smell of coffee reminds the smell of excrement while the smell of tea reminds the smell of incense and marihuana.

Coffee, in postmodern culture, is mirrored by *Coke* (not only the name and the color are the same!) while the subtle wisdom of tea has no parallel in postmodern culture.

To conclude it has no place in it. On my recent travel to South America I was in midst of the coffee culture and guess it, did not like it. I thus settled among the tea drinkers, on the other half of the globe and leave it over to Freudian analysts to find out why Westerners like the smell of excrement and toilet paper, while in Asia you have a toilet shower, or just a bucket with water, even in a very simple toilet. That's why coffee and Christianity is also related to dirty asses while in Asia people smell good not only on the upper half of their body.

And the latter is again a metaphor as the body *talks*. The way we treat the body, the way we treat the mind. It's logical that drinking a gall-bitter black soup and run around toilet-papered results in a mind that is dirty from top to toes.

When you drink wisdom and shower your ass after toilet, you are *ready for sex anytime, anywhere, anyhow.* You are ready for heaven, then, and your mind is clear like a morning in Darjeeling …

Sex Therapy

Narcissism is like the wood puppets on strings that you move by moving the strings. The narcissistic boy is moved by his mother moving the strings, the narcissistic girl is moved by her father moving the strings. To end narcissism means to cut off the strings and let the wood limbs move freely by their own weight or else the air, or somebody touching them.

The *wisdom of narcissism* is to learn that we can get away from a puppet life and head into a real life where our limbs are not moved by strings but by our own muscles. In turn, it is true that our muscles are moved not by strings but by our own bioenergy.

To conclude, to end narcissism means to strengthen this bioenergetic force by putting an end to the eternal copulation with parental energies. It is to fuck off the string mover and send your *symbiotoholic* Mom or Dad to hell.

It is to move our limbs by ourselves. Doing this, the puppet becomes a living human, fully autonomous and no more entrapped in a string life.

Narcissism is a wound that can be healed by taking away bioenergy from it and investing that bioenergy into our *life's mission*. The narcissistic wound has only power over us *as long as we comply with something*, but as we end complying-with and begin acting on our limbs, its pattern is broken.

Narcissism is a pattern that works only in string societies, which are societies where the moral setup demands compliance and thus over-adaptation to a concept valid for all.

To see this *means to affirm our individuality* and our soul power to get to move freely within our continuum and not outside of it, and so we can really break this pattern apart.

The solution, thus, is unconditional self-affirmation.

THE MURDER HERO

When you travel around the world, you become aware, if you are not already, to what point what we call *modern culture* is rooting out the last bit of innocence and joy of life even in the most remote villages around the globe.

You have to travel really to far remote places, virtually into the jungle, high into least accessible mountains or to the poles of the globe to find peoples that are still little affected by the cultural and physical genocide that the murder culture is carrying out, with ruthless precision, like a gradual overkill of all living on earth. Is that astonishing after all?

I think it's in the logic of a dead society to seek out making the world save for *death*. This, then, seems to be the mission of the white dominant culture that is one where murder is the order of the day and where *serious entertainment*, made in the most heroic of all countries, is all about the *Murder Hero*.

Most of us are *dulled and pacified* into aloofness, and our critical sense has been castrated, first through the *emotional death* we have suffered in childhood, second through the intellectual and neurotic overdrive in which we are in as a *compensation* for the connectedness we lost, third through the constant mass media manipulation we are too weak or too lazy to resist. It is a deep fatal error to think that all this is a *modern* phenomenon. The analysis of human evolution clearly shows that the present worldwide murder culture has its roots in our last five thousand years of patriarchal history. In fact, it is naïve and ignorant to believe anything in nature or in the human-created world could come about in a vacuum.

The present multi-faceted, cross-cultural and institutionalized murders are based upon a murder tradition that goes back to the *Code of Hammurabi.* In killing the pleasure function and submitting it to group supervision and control, the human race has signed a contract with the devil, after having created this devil as a split-off self that controls the controller. It is equally naïve and ignorant to believe that the present catastrophic state of affairs could have come about through any specific religion or ideology.

While still decades ago, the human masses were so ignorant to believe that most ideologies were necessary or even *god-given,* many today begin to question this. But instead of seeing the failure of all ideologies for the advancement of mankind, *they blame particular ideologies while upholding others.*

The Bible is very explicit in favoring the *in-group* and excluding the *out-group,* and murder was not only permitted by even ordained by the cultural divinity, Yahweh, when there was a need to advance in one's business through domination and the ruthless massacre of those that were naturally opposing such domination.

Yahweh is the ultimate *Murder Hero* and, as such, the immediate predecessor of our modern Hitlers, Mussolinis, Perons, Chomeinis and Saddam Husseins. Today's short-sighted Western credo is that Islamic culture was to blame for the terrible disorder in the world. This assumption overlooks that Islam shares with Christianity and Judaism the same base paradigm and murderous ideology that promises *Heil* and human advancement based upon the rape-and-repression of nature, oligarchic control and the hypertrophy of *yang* to the detriment of *yin*. This terrible lie, that is by itself the root of murder, has been paid with innumerable victims, in the past, and today, and it has caused humanity to retrograde in its evolution. We have not advanced one little bit since the time, far in pre-history, when the natural order still reigned or, as the Chinese sages say, when the Tao was still honored and preserved.

We have neither advanced through one-sided and inhuman technological progress, nor through any of the many *betterments* that saviors and ideologies offered us as a remedy of the mess that they themselves have contributed to create.

We are still in the adolescence of humanity and most of our collective endeavors to *root out evil* through returning to old and integrated strategies are but immature attempts to clean up a mess that today no human can ever totally understand, so immense it is.

We have created total confusion in our relationships, and put the love principle upside-down, demonized what is naturally beautiful and enriching and put up *false values* that render us shallow and mean, and full of suspicion and fear.

To justify what we see is producing still more confusion and destruction, and in order to veil our millenary stupidity, we blame nature and human nature.

While it is so obvious that it's the *perversion of nature* and human nature that has created the mess and brings about the destruction, but not this nature herself, we go on affirming that nature was wrong and not to be trusted and our so-called *scientific* mind could *correct the errors inherent in nature.*

No murder can happen without being preceded by a murder *inside of us* way before we set out to kill. The very desire to kill comes about through the schizoid split that *killing something within ourselves* brought about. Our past millennia of collective murder and genocide were preceded by killing one of our internal opposites and thus upsetting the natural balance of *yin* and *yang* within us: by condemning and highly regulating *sexual pleasure* or certain forms of it, by achieving to regulate and repress the *natural flow of the emotional and sexual energies in the lives of our children*, we have deeply interfered in the natural order of things, and have turned upside-down the flow of the bioenergy, not only in the human being but, as all is connected, also in the *stratosphere* of the earth, in the *planetary energies* within our galaxy and the *intergalactic energy* balance within the whole of the cosmos. And we had no right doing so because the bodies of our children are not our bodies, as we do *not own* our bodies.

The human body as the whole of life cannot be owned. Lao-tzu said that the human body is the eternal adaptability of heaven. Other philosophers said that the universe or mother earth lends us a body that we have to give back when we die.

In fact, even the dullest of the dull must admit that we cannot take our bodies into the afterlife. Minutes after our spirit has left our body, this body begins to decay and in a few days is but a peace of rotten flesh that is virtually eaten up by a multitude of birds, insects, worms, beetles and other animals and plants that mother earth sends out to embrace back in her substance what she has so generously granted us as a vehicle for our spiritual advancement.

Life is created by pleasure and natural death equally is *pleasure* as it opens an illuminated path into a more subtle and less dense *vibrational* existence.

Killing natural loving attraction, and destroying friendships was the foremost tool of dominator culture to get hold of humans and to manipulate and control them into the literal essence of their flesh and their bones.

By the same token and with the same goal, dominator culture repressed the truth about the cyclic nature of birth-and-death, and invented the myth of a *linear one-time life* that ended in death as a form of ultimate shock and destruction.

The three dominator religions that I mentioned above have coincided in suppressing the teaching of reincarnation that is an essential element of perennial philosophy.

By distorting *emotional and sexual complexity* in the development of children and inculcating fear in the masses of their believers by the presumption that only religious saviors had the *key to heaven* in their hands, the avatars of these religious ideologies have put up the foundation for not only the tortures, massacres and genocide to occur against various out-groups, but also those that were committed by the cultures that succeeded those first examples of a dehumanized species that not for nothing is called *mankind* and not *womankind*.

For without attacking and attempting to destroy the *yin* principle in nature and rendering the female a slave to man, the wisdom contained in the female principle *would not have permitted* the murder culture to raise to worldwide dominion.

That is why the fight of man against nature *was and is synonymous with man fighting woman*, or, to express it in energetic terms, an upset and hypertrophied *yang* trying to subdue a demonized *yin* in order to gain *absolute control* over all living.

Upside Down

I question what I clearly recognize, by intelligent observation, as an *upside-down movement* or perversion from the laws of life. Children who are *pure and innocent* are such a perversion. And I have seen hyperactive and pre-psychotic children invariably being raised in that kind of environment.

Let me explain what I mean by upside-down movement. I see an upside-down movement from life when people are up to define as sex naked corps à corps with a prepubescent child; to label *child abuser* a modern body-conscious educator who is hands-on; to hold healthy a child that is unorgasmic and has no sexual appetite; to assess as *normal* children that are water-headed, insomniac, and hyperactive; to find it natural when male children sadistically mistreat female children; to find it blameless that publicity exploits its creation: the consumer child; to find it *nice and funny* when fat consumer children sing idiotic songs at idiotic birthday parties; to hold it necessary to exclude male day care teachers from body care; to find it *good and decent* to separate boys and girls in school; to judge *unthinkable* the idea to give children a complete love education; to educate children by *teaching values* instead of the laws of life; to recruit educators from the mainstream bulk of educastrated idiots; to justify as *inevitable* child rape in war and civil war; to endorse physical child abuse while being against sexual child abuse; to find it *good and healthy* when children are emotionally and sexually starved; to judge a little girl *a good girl* when in reality she is totally frigid; to have nothing against the fact that most children receive a fake education; to love dogs and pets more than children and adolescents; to have children killed, mutilated and rendered orphans in wars and civil wars; and finally, to judge all the preceding *a cunning journalistic trick for justifying or normalizing pedophilia.*

The Admin Hero

Some of our modern functionaries, perhaps conscious of the mass murder, destruction and misery that a few thousand years of patriarchy have brought about, are now to face a complex network of problems that are all interwoven with each other.

They ask for the *Admin Hero*.

Perhaps for the first time in human history, other than tribal cultures, and even some circles of dominator cultures are building a sad awareness of the mess we are facing, at the present moment, only two years from the end of human history as predicted by the Mayan calendar.

But in a mood of fatalistic *tristezza*, these functionaries, politicians and economic decision makers have for the most part become mere *administrators* of our global problems; and this simply because, while the solutions of most issues can be found using top-notch probability calculation, quantum science insights and simple human intuition, the point where things become stuck is in most instances the *political agenda*.

As a result, instead of using their energies and zeal for bringing about necessary change in the jungle of worldwide problem networks from hunger, over war and air pollution to deforestation and desertification, these functionaries invest their time and resources in the mere *administration of problems*.

Problem A is redefined as problem B so that problem A can be traced from the political agenda, after peacefully going underground and *reappearing* in the new costume of problem B that is proudly presented to the masses as a *new problem*.

Problem C is declared as a problem typical for regime X and thus no more existing under regime Y.

Problem D is declared unsolvable because it does not fall into the responsibility of any state government, while international government, because it does not exist yet, cannot be accounted for solving the problem.

Problem E is declared a problem of lacking financial resources and thus stored away in the *unsolvables* drawer, using the scarcity paradigm as a justification for non-action instead of using appropriate means to raise the necessary funds.

Problem F is put on the back of a particular human or a group that serves as a scapegoat to be slaughtered for veiling its true originators.

Problem G is renamed problem X and problem X is renamed problem G because this operation fits in a particular political agenda, thus raising the public confusion even further.

Problem H is a *matter of competence* and found unsolvable because the *right competence* could not be found.

I leave it up to you to find the *appropriate real-life examples* that I intentionally left out in order to stimulate your imagination and creative cooperation in bringing about the ultimate shared experience of this writing. It is really easy to find numerous examples that give flesh to the *cunning schemes of political manipulation* that I cited above, and that are by no means exhaustive.

Leaving it over to more or less corrupt, mediocre, uncreative or even utterly stupid politicians to solve our worldwide problems, we face that with every year, contrary to what we hear in the media, our problems rise and our living standard and life quality falls.

With every new day, we are more indebted to the murderous strategies of worldwide corporations and lesser free to find and realize viable alternatives.

Many of us have accepted as part of *normal life* that most of our larger cities worldwide are hopelessly jammed with traffic and buried under acid rain most of the year, crammed with garbage and ruins once we leave the clean-and-glorious city centers and extend our view into the suburbs. Most of us find it normal that at day we look into the halogen-lit shop windows of noble fashion or design boutiques and at night stumble over anonymous bodies of homeless people next to huge black garbage bags that *incarnate the shadow* of our glorious murder culture.

And this experience, you have it today in New York as well as in Sao Paolo, in Los Angeles as well as in Shanghai, in Berlin as well as in Paris, in Manila as well as in Mexico City or Delhi.

Most of us accept that our children's souls slowly die and that their bodies are robbed and their pleasures destroyed in the *child prisons* that we call *schools* and that are the only prisons where absolutely no human rights ever penetrated.

Most of us find it normal that while females have fought their way into decision-making, the females that did so *have betrayed their womanhood* and all that it implies, and have become the worst vintages of perverted males that ever existed.

Most of us find it normal *that in early child care there are as good as no more males* because males have been labeled *abusers-in-spe* by the new dominator agenda of feminism that spreads like a modern-day virus of *abused* feminity perverted into violent fundamentalism on a worldwide scale.

Most of us find it normal that every year military budgets are raised while educational budgets are cut, that every day more streets are built for cars we do neither need nor want. In one word, most of us find it normal that our problems are well administered instead of at least badly solved.

Let the Children Play

The only and true child abuse is the one that is *daily committed* by well-meaning and system-conform parents and that, needless to add, goes totally unnoticed and unpatrolled. It is the child abuse in the name of the *best of the child.* It is the child abuse committed in the name of *sacred traditions* that have covered this green globe with a black veil, suffocating real life and real love under its stigmatizing views and *moral* opinions.

True morality in matters of child education is first of all based on respecting the child's intrinsic erotic nature and by the practice of non-interference in the child's natural sphere of intimacy, which includes respect of their friendships and all that hairy folk around children who grow up *unregulated*.

It is to leave their poetic little world as untouched as possible, and contemplating it as an enrichment to our busy impoverished adult lives. As Bob Marley so wonderfully said it in his famous song: *Let the children play*.

How many times in your life have you met a little girl that was ready for all, so sweet, so yielding, so totally devoted to give herself fully to life, without fear, without apprehension, and without *morality*?

Michel Petruccianni has expressed this magic of love in his song *The Prayer*, rendered beautifully in his *Blue Note Recordings*. I have nothing to add to this unique description of love for life, put in a musical prayer. I can only bow in front of so much wisdom! My story continues.

The girl was transformed the next day. Because there was grandmother, and the usual small talk. And because the story that grandmother deployed *was a lie through and through.*

She wanted to fetch me as a husband. Period. Ultimate reason. Strategic move. Love chess. On the back of a child that was put *in the frontline.* A child used as a fishing device.

But the fish escaped.

THE LOVE HERO

There is a *new culture* raising especially in highly civilized societies that refuses to stay with analyzing and blaming the terrible state of affairs we are in, and instead practices a new way of living.

While these movements are very diverse and sometimes hard to define in mere verbal terms, what they have in common is that they attempt to become *germs* or *living cells* of what could be realized on a larger scale within a new human, and truly humane, society and culture. While the first ecological communities were founded already in the 1960s and the movement as a whole not surviving, the basic idea is familiar with all those who practice one or the other alternative lifestyle. Young people today who subscribe to what could be called a *love culture* seem to be inspired by a deep quest for innocence. They wait for the *Love Hero* to manifest.

They are often working in professions that either involve art, drama, dance and music, or the professions that deal with natural healing, body work, healthy diet and integral living, or else they are *unconventional* psychiatrists or psychoanalysts, astrologers or numerologists as well as those who engage in one or the other spiritual path such as Yoga or Zen. We can realize powerful new solutions by just doing things *positively* instead of criticizing and analyzing things and events that were and are negative.

This insight contributed to his change.

He had become a *love hero* after stripping off his old serpent skins. He was looking at the world with other eyes. He was changing his *regard*. The hateful expression had vanished from his eyes. And as he left his dull and abusive childhood behind, declaring it *wasteland*, and set his sights high, to look over the fence, in a new landscape of potentiality, and as a result of the insights he got through analysis and intuition, and through the skill of expressing them in writing, he was able to leave the phase of revolt and enter his inner world of bliss. And life blessed him with healing and consolation once he had taken the decision to change his worldview and throw out all the old garbage that had transformed his world into a mess of broken glass and bleeding feet.

And once of a sudden, he felt that his inner tension gave rise to a new and hitherto *unheard-of sense of latitude*. He was looking virtually through new eyes, and while the world that he saw was basically the same, the observer had changed. He had not changed thinking, but *the thinker* – and that was a true psychological revolution. He felt at peace with the world, and as it was, and how terrible it was or not, and he did *not need to change it*.

He then also realized that he did not need to alter himself and could accept himself as he was – imperfect and yet a creature energized by love, and not by hate. While he had set out to write a large study about the murder culture and all its effects in human history and today's global culture, he then saw that he needed not the effort for saying what needed to be said.

He then also saw that to see only murder and destruction would be one-sided and only reflect *one aspect* of the Tao, while the other, *regeneration and new creation* was to be seen and valued as well.

This, eventually, led him to the insight that as faster and harder mainstream murder culture pushes ahead, the faster and the more effective *the new love culture* will be born into existence and begin to find larger and larger circles of adherents and *life lovers* by conviction.

During his almost twenty-year long addiction to hate and revolt, *he learnt that nothing is more destructive for oneself than to wanting to change the world,* and that such an endeavor is truly schizophrenic. The world changes by itself, as a child grows without strings to pull him up. The world is what we see of it, what we project on it, what we can *digest* of it.

If it is true that the hater will at the end of the day be devoured by his hatred, and the judger shall be judged on the lines of his own rigid judgments, the lover of the world and seeker of truth who *embraces the world,* being one with his Tao and *tolerating the uneducated and foolish* as says the I Ching, will endure.

And thus he saw that *all was good*, as his own change will inevitably bring about gradual change *on a larger and transpersonal scale* and with larger support from all walks of global society.